Dr K M A Ahamed Zubair

Thirsty Caravan: Exploring the Perpetual Search for Love in Narratives

Dr K M A Ahamed Zubair

Thirsty Caravan: Exploring the Perpetual Search for Love in Narratives

Dr. Sanaa Sha'lan's Arabic Short Story Collection: Examining Gender Dynamics and Societal Symbolism in Qafila al-'Athsh

Noor Publishing

Imprint

Any brand names and product names mentioned in this book are subject to trademark, brand or patent protection and are trademarks or registered trademarks of their respective holders. The use of brand names, product names, common names, trade names, product descriptions etc. even without a particular marking in this work is in no way to be construed to mean that such names may be regarded as unrestricted in respect of trademark and brand protection legislation and could thus be used by anyone.

Cover image: www.ingimage.com

Publisher:
Noor Publishing
is a trademark of
Dodo Books Indian Ocean Ltd. and OmniScriptum S.R.L publishing group

120 High Road, East Finchley, London, N2 9ED, United Kingdom
Str. Armeneasca 28/1, office 1, Chisinau MD-2012, Republic of Moldova, Europe
Printed at: see last page
ISBN: 978-620-7-47858-3

Thirsty Caravan: Exploring the Perpetual Search for Love in Narratives

Dr. Sanaa Sha'lan's Arabic Short Story Collection: Examining Gender Dynamics and Societal Symbolism in *Qafila al-'Athsh*

Dr.K.M.A.Ahamed Zubair

Associate Professor of Arabic, The New College, Chennai 600 014, India

اللغة العربية تحمل كلمة الله، وروح محمد ﷺ، وسر الإسلام،

This work has been dedicated to the Indian Islamic Missionaries (1500-1800)

Preface

The power of storytelling lies not just in the tale itself, but in the layers of depth it unravels. Sanaa al-Shaalan's "Thirst Caravan" is a tapestry of symbolism, ideology, and societal commentary woven into the intricate fabric of a narrative set against the harsh desert backdrop. This essay aims to dissect the thematic elements, delve into the narrative nuances, and uncover the profound implications embedded within the text.

"Caravan of Thirst" by Sanaa Al Shaalan is a literary expedition into the intricate emotions, fervent desires, and profound human connections woven intricately across fifteen compelling narratives. Each story within this collection encapsulates a distinctive facet of the human experience, delving into the multifaceted nature of longing, love, and the ceaseless pursuit of fulfillment. These tales traverse the labyrinth of emotions, inviting readers to explore the depths of human desires and the eternal quest for contentment

Dr K M A Ahamed Zubair

Contents

Introduction
"Thirst Caravan" by Sanaa al-Shaalan is a narrative that transcends the boundaries of storytelling, weaving together a rich tapestry of thematic intricacies and cultural reflections. This essay ventures into the heart of the story, dissecting its symbolism, exploring the clash of ideologies, and uncovering the subtle nuances that speak volumes about societal norms and individual struggles within the Arab context.

The setting, a harsh desert landscape, becomes more than just a backdrop—it serves as a canvas upon which the societal injustices, traditions, and struggles are vividly portrayed. Through a careful analysis of the temporal context, dialogues, narrative perspective, and stylistic choices, this essay aims to peel back the layers of the narrative, revealing the profound themes and insights imbibed within "Thirst Caravan."

In "Caravan of Thirst," Sanaa Al Shaalan crafts a mosaic of narratives that traverse the landscapes of human emotions, relationships, and the incessant yearning for love. The collection commences with "Caravan of Thirst," a story emblematic of societal constraints and the resilience of femininity amid the constraints of societal norms. This narrative lays the groundwork, enveloping readers within a world teeming with unmet yearnings and restrained desires.

Subsequent tales like "A Message to God," "The Rag," and "Heart for All Bodies" intricately thread the emotional tapestry, depicting the desperation, rejection, and the search for pure love. Each story, crafted with poignant prose and evocative imagery, peels back layers of human vulnerability, revealing the intricate complexities of the heart's desires.

The collection culminates with "The Envy," a story that echoes the overarching theme of eternal pursuit, leaving readers introspecting about the never-ending quest for the ideal, the unattainable, and the enduring hope for fulfillment.

Sanaa Al-Shala'an and the Story of the *Thirst Caravan*

Study of the story ("Thirst Caravan"):

The story of the "Thirst Caravan" opens up a range of intellectual, cultural, and social dimensions of our Arab society. It's a narrative of great flexibility, interpreted by the reader from various angles. The storyteller hails from an environment that oppressed women's rights for decades. However, voices arose condemning this injustice and striving to restore what was taken from women intentionally or unintentionally. This story becomes one of those eager cries to restore women's true value in our Arab world.

Summary of the story's events:

Set in the desert, the story depicts a Ghazi tribe defeating another tribe and capturing their women. The leader of the victorious tribe falls in love with one of the captives, seemingly the daughter of the defeated tribe's leader. He refuses the defeated tribe's offer to ransom the women with money, instead honoring the girl he loves by granting them freedom. The victorious tribe also provides food and water. The climax occurs when the beautiful captive girl, contrary to expectations, rejects leaving her captor and chooses to stay with him, defying societal norms and obstacles to achieve her feminine freedom. The story ends with the caravan's return, laden with shame due to the impact of the girl's actions on their honor. Men of the tribe, upon returning, kill their women out of thirst witnessed in their eyes, fearing they might bring shame as the heroine did in the text.

The main theme of the story:

The narrative's foundation rests on two opposing intellectual currents: one supportive of women's legitimate demands, seeking liberation from detrimental beliefs and negative thoughts that regress them to antiquated customs (represented by the Bedouin movement), and the other condemning earnest efforts to liberate women from the cruelty of prevailing customs and traditions, hindering any progress in women's empowerment (portrayed by the men of the Thirst Caravan). This structure unveils the author's intended significance.

The significance of the title "Thirst Caravan":

The title is pivotal in any literary work, serving as the procedural key where the creative components converge, focusing on the condensed state of events within the narrative structure. It also reveals cultural, social, intellectual, and psychological aspects forming the story's foundation. The title portrays the caravan as primarily carrying water in the desert. However, the addition of "thirst" creates reader intrigue, prompting questions about the author's purpose. It highlights the fundamental duality within the story, dominating it from the title to its conclusion.

The "thirst" symbolizes women's yearning and longing for their rights, aspirations, and hopes stolen by a society that saw women merely as tools for men's emotions and reproduction. It signifies the woman's need for her rights, as essential to her life and existence as water is to humanity, presenting a realistic social critique of women's rights in our Arab world.

The focal points in the story:

The dark Bedouin, from the negative perspective, represents the oppressors who strip women of their freedom and dignity.

Yet, from the standpoint of determined women seeking change, he becomes the liberator and savior, akin to a straw for a drowning person to reach safety.

The women who boarded the Thirst Caravan, believing it was for their redemption, are the ones rejecting any portrayal of a new image for women. They prefer staying and returning to what was, out of fear of the unknown future. They represent the feminist current trapped behind walls of fear, ignorance, and limited options.

The beautiful captive girl, choosing to remain with her captor, symbolizes the feminist movement demanding their rights and seeking to create a new reality for Arab women in all its aspects. This movement embodies women in their most empowered forms—assertive, beautiful, rejecting, and captivating simultaneously. These contradictions for women forged an active and contrasting existence, unlike what society knew of them, projecting only one dimension, not beyond the negative expectations.

What's striking in this story is the dominance of individual values over communal values. The dark Bedouin (the captor) represents a contradictory current against the group of men who came to reclaim the women. The beautiful woman (the captive) symbolizes a contrasting current against the group of women who boarded the Thirst Caravan to return to their previous state. This indicates that as an Arab society, we're still at the beginning of a path towards accepting a new image or reality for Arab women. The positive individual versus the negative collective suggests that the vast majority still resists and isn't entirely capable of embracing the full scope of change.

Primary Characters:
A. Main characters: The story revolves around two pivotal characters: the dark Bedouin and the beautiful captive girl.

The dark Bedouin: A strong, brave character capable of defending her ideas, seeing a better future in the new things coming. She refuses the oppression of women and the suppression of their freedom. This character represents the supportive male current for women, advocating for their defense and recognition, favored by women themselves. The beautiful captive girl: A central rebellious character against the reality of women's lives in the Arab world, rejecting it. Assertive and aspiring to achieve the best in her feminine world deprived of much since ancient times, events drove her towards unexpected and bizarre paths. She sought to impose a new reality holding a better vision and a deeper insight, centered on the complementarity of men and women in our Arab societies.

B. Secondary characters:

The tribe's elder represents a steadfast character in their beliefs, not inclined towards change or renewal, preferring to stay under harsh, oppressive traditions that deny women any value or consideration. They view women as devoid of will, always under men's control. Yet, he's surprised by his daughter breaking the boundaries of his expectations and tribe, persistently striving for the pinnacle of feminine human freedom, forming her own identity and world.

The men of the tribe represent the ignorant view of women, shown in their killing of their young daughters upon the caravan's return, symbolizing the killing of those dreams and hopes before they materialize.

The young girls symbolize the oppressed, innocent figures, faultless yet fated to grow up dreaming of possessing their stolen world.

The Setting:

The author chose the desert as the backdrop for the events, not randomly but for its deep symbolism woven into the story's narrative structure. The desert embodies deprivation, loss, and negation, holding no value for women in that environment.

The author's intentional choice of this setting aligns with the story's intentions for two reasons: First, the desert's harsh, dry nature parallels the severity of Arab traditions and customs, highlighting their oppression of women's rights. Second, the desert being the original homeland of the Arabs suggests that this is the ancient Arab view of women. The Arabs still cling to their traditions inherited from tribal days.

Time:
In the Thirst Caravan, time is condensed into the

day the caravan came to reclaim its captives, filled with surprises on both cultural and civilized levels for the tribe's men. It ends with the tribe's sorrowful lament in the evening. Generally, the story's time refers us to the pre-Islamic era, where burying baby girls became a "cruel ritual." This era aligns with the main theme, highlighting the lack of value for women and the unjust treatment they've received historically.

Dialogue:

The dialogue reveals each character's intellectual stance in the story. For instance, the conversation between the tribal leader and the dark Bedouin exposes the ideological opposition each stands for. Similarly, the dialogue between the dark Bedouin and the beautiful girl illustrates the nature of the stance and cognitive current favored by women. These dialogues align with the central theme more clearly, allowing the narrator to persuade the reader.

The Narrator:

The narrator assumes the role of a knowledgeable storyteller, revealing her inclination towards individual values over communal ones from the story's start. She criticizes the tribe and rejects its concepts and beliefs. The narrator's intervention through commentary and description further emphasizes her preconceived bias against the tribe, establishing her alignment with individual values in contrast to tribal values.

The Plot:

The plot becomes evident when the girl refuses to return to her family and tribe, preferring captivity over them. This rejection disrupts the expectations of her father, tribe, and the reader, adding beauty to the story. If she had returned, it would have been a familiar, conventional outcome, thus stepping beyond the confines of a typical narrative.

Language and Style:

The author's language employs classical Arabic, free from colloquialisms, while the expressions used carry symbolic meanings without sliding into direct interpretations. The language is condensed, poetic, carrying a multitude of artistic images that serve the story's purpose. Additionally, the author utilizes Arabic heritage, as seen in the reference to burying girls, enhancing the text's aesthetic and symbolic dimensions.

The writer adheres to refined Arabic language and literature, avoiding colloquial language and integrating a poetic style, allowing for a narrative treatment that preserves the literary aspect, steering clear of falling into the story's pitfall. Concerning style, the narrative's expansion contrasts with the reduction in dialogue, indicating a flaw in human relationships within this desert setting. The reduction of dialogue implies an inability to communicate between genders, where males dictate what they deem appropriate while females execute without discussion. This stylistic technique also serves the story's primary purpose by casting light on repression, deprivation, and silencing within the narrative.

:

.

Analyzing Themes and Elements in "Thirst Caravan" by Sanaa al-Shaalan

Sanaa al-Shaalan's "Thirst Caravan" intricately weaves together a narrative rich in thematic depth, symbolism, and stylistic elements. Exploring the plight of women within the harsh, unforgiving desert landscape, the story unveils societal norms, the clash of ideologies, and the struggle for individuality against oppressive traditions.

Setting as Symbolism

The deliberate choice of the desert as the story's backdrop mirrors the cruelty of Arab customs, mirroring their historical oppression of women. This setting serves as a metaphor for the dry, barren nature of traditions, rigid and unyielding like the harsh desert environment. Furthermore, the desert being the homeland of the Arabs symbolizes an ancient perspective on women, portraying the enduring grip of tribal traditions that have persisted through generations.

Temporal Context: Pre-Islamic Era

The narrative unfolds within a condensed timeframe, primarily focused on the day the Thirst Caravan arrives to reclaim its captives. This setting in a pre-Islamic era amplifies the theme of the devaluation of women, vividly depicted through the burial of infant girls as a "cruel ritual." This temporal context emphasizes the historical injustice and lack of recognition for women's rights, entrenched within societal norms.

Dialogues as Ideological Showcases
Conversations between characters unveil ideological conflicts and societal perspectives. The dialogue between the tribal leader and the dark Bedouin reflects contrasting ideological stands, while the interaction between the Bedouin and the beautiful girl illuminates the cognitive currents favored by women. These dialogues serve as mirrors reflecting the clash between different worldviews, accentuating the struggle for individuality within the collective societal framework.

Narrative Perspective: The Author's Voice
The narrative voice assumes an omniscient role, guiding readers through the events while implicitly criticizing tribal norms and values. By rejecting the tribe's ideologies, the narrator underscores an alignment with individualistic values, emphasizing a subtle critique of societal structures and the imbalance of power.

Plot: Defying Expectations
The story's plot subverts conventional expectations when the girl refuses to return to her family and tribe, choosing captivity instead. This narrative choice adds complexity and depth to the storyline, challenging readers' preconceived notions and adding an unexpected layer of empowerment to the female protagonist.

Language and Style: Poetic Expression and Cultural Heritage
Al-Shaalan employs refined Arabic language, devoid of colloquialisms, carrying symbolic nuances and poetic expressions. Her use of Arabic cultural heritage, notably in the reference to the ritualistic burial of infant girls, enhances the narrative's aesthetic and adds layers of cultural and symbolic significance.

In conclusion, "Thirst Caravan" encapsulates a multifaceted portrayal of societal norms, gender roles, and the struggle for autonomy within a deeply entrenched traditional Arab society. Through its thematic depth, symbolic setting, nuanced dialogues, and narrative style, the story echoes the ongoing struggle for individuality and the challenges faced by women in societies dictated by rigid norms and traditions.

Conclusion

In the intricate tapestry of "Thirst Caravan," Sanaa al-Shaalan crafts a narrative that transcends the boundaries of time and tradition. Through the barren yet potent setting of the desert, she paints a vivid picture of societal norms, the clash between individual autonomy and collective traditions, and the struggle for recognition within a patriarchal structure.

The story's profound symbolism, mirrored in the harshness of the desert, the nuanced dialogues, and the author's omniscient voice, speaks volumes about the enduring struggle of women in Arab society. "Thirst Caravan" stands not just as a story but as a profound commentary on the complexities of societal expectations, individual autonomy, and the quest for empowerment. As the narrative unfolds, it leaves an indelible imprint, inviting readers to contemplate the intricate layers of human existence and societal constructs embedded within its pages.

The Aesthetics of Titles in Sanaa Al-Shaalan's Stories: The Thirst Caravan Collection as an Example

The title is a fundamental cornerstone in literary work, serving as the procedural key where the components of the creative work converge. It gathers the elements forming the creative work's structure, guiding the reader towards the condensed core of the narrative within the textual framework. Through this focal point, the reader's perspectives unfold, revealing the aesthetic connection between the literary work's title and the sequence of events within it.

Titles hold significant importance in literary production, representing a condensed image conveying the narrative's essence through hints and signals that intertwine, akin to a spider's web, placing the reader in an interactive experience with the literary text. This interactive experience involves a series of reading procedures, commencing with the title and culminating in the conclusion of the literary work. Thus, the reader encounters a new creative vision by engaging with the literary text starting from its title.

The title acts as the initial threshold and simultaneously the ultimate boundary where the reader delves into the text, discovering the inherent beauty unveiled by the title. It embodies the circular motion of the literary work, being both the starting point and the conclusion. Notably, the importance of titles in literary creation extends beyond modern and contemporary literature, as evident in the attention ancient Arab critics paid to titles in their writings, emphasizing their significance.

Historically, figures like Abu Bakr Al-Suli highlighted the role of titles as a defining identity for a literary work. Similarly, Abu Al-Qasim Muhammad ibn Abdul Ghafur Al-Kalai elaborated on the importance of titles as indicators of the content and substance of a piece, signifying the engagement and interaction between the reader, the text, and the subsequent exploration of the aesthetic value hinted at by the title.

Ultimately, a good writer selects titles that engage the reader's mind, making them interactive with the literary work from the first glance at the title. Al-Kalai reasoned that the title could be named based on two aspects: signifying the purpose of the book or simply because it represents and encapsulates the essence of the written material itself.

"And to whom it is intended! The first aspect refers to the content and essence of the book, while the second aspect encompasses the textual message's sender and receiver. Here, with Al-Kalai, we find a comprehensive vision of the creative process, which includes three fundamental pillars: the message, the sender, and the receiver.

The term 'title' may typically refer to the subject of the book, much like an 'address.' Therefore, it's evident from our earlier discussion that the title wasn't isolated from critical vision in Arab culture. Arab culture, with its diverse components, carried an image of evolution in its finest forms in ancient times. The perspectives of ancient critics were comprehensive towards literary and cultural output, including their evolved view of titles, reaching its peak in modern eras.

It can be said that titles in Arabic literature underwent an evolutionary phase since the early Islamic era. Four factors converged to facilitate title evolution, prominently seen in the fields of recording Islamic human thought during the flourishing Islamic civilization. These factors, intertwined and converged, represented the flourishing image of Arab culture. They contributed to the development of titling directly connected to the Arab culture, which reached its pinnacle during the Abbasid era.

After this brief insight into the concept of the title, it's essential to delve into the aesthetic elements of reading the title in literary text. No writer or author can randomly choose a title for their literary work; it holds significant intentionality. Creative writing, inherently, is far from innocence; there are no innocent texts. Texts seek, through the creator's thoughts and emotions, to provoke the reader. However, it's not hostile provocation but a means to unveil the text's beauty in all its details, including the title, which serves as the initial starting point to reveal the concealed within the text.

Therefore, the aesthetics of receiving the title stand as a measure, in one way or another, of the gap's narrowness or breadth between the title and the text. Thus, reading seeks to establish a relationship between the two ends to fill this gap. This is accomplished by the reader's engagement in unraveling the condensation dominating the title through interpretative mechanisms and comprehension achieved through objective interaction between the text's elements and the reader's culture.

Hence, we're facing a dialectical discourse between the two parties (the text and the reader). When we mention the text, we refer to all its associations, including the creator, because writing is a companion to absence (the absence of the speaker) and the disconnection and rupture, even death, from the source. Therefore, this situation signifies an impact on the spatial-temporal relationship - titling, comprising the text's name and its creator, becomes the symbolic or semiotic compensation for the presence that existed and suddenly vanished at the moment of text production (the speech event). The title thus becomes the objective equivalent of both the creator and the text, carrying imprints of the text, which in turn embodies the imprints of the creator who produced it.

I believe that in the moment of choosing a fitting title for their work, the creator ascends to a moment of transcendence. They invoke in their mind all the strands of the text and its focal points, leading them to produce another text more condensed than the one narrated. Isn't it the title, as a general reading threshold, crucial as it represents the first encounter in the reader's journey? It gives a general impression of the text's significances and signifies a double threshold intended to carry numerous meanings and symbols, serving as the first gateway through which the reader enters the literary text. The title is an effective tool in communicating with the reader, bearing within it the text's essence and inspiring curiosity and a desire to explore what lies behind it. It mirrors artistic condensation and a well-crafted creative vision that captivates the reader's attention and drives them towards discovering the text's worlds and beauties."

The functions of the title encompass condensation, implication, and an eloquent invitation to read. It opens broad horizons for interpretation and reveals the interconnected aesthetic aspects between the title and the structure of the text. This interaction evolves into a dialogic relationship through interwoven themes in the literary work's title and its structure. The participants in this dialogic relationship are the reader and the creator. The emergence of the title signifies its dominance and compels both the creator and the reader. The former, as the leader and pioneer in the text, and the latter, as the one overshadowed by its authority, seeking permission to enter the world of the text. When the reader enters the spaces of the title, expansive interpretative avenues unfold, granting insight into the artistic elements of the title's structure.

The title of the short story collection:

The title of any short story collection serves as the fundamental axis around which the events of the stories within it revolve. The title chosen by the writer becomes the key to the collection, containing a silky thread that connects the events of the story to those of other stories within the collection. It's noteworthy for any perceptive reader of literary works to discern the significance of an author's choice of a specific title within the collection's titles. This choice reveals the depth behind the selection, signifying a significant turning point in the writer's emotional and artistic experience. The collection chosen by the writer to be the magical key through its title allows readers to delve into the cultural, social, ideological, and psychological elements embedded within the stories. Taking Sanaa Al-Shalan's "Caravan of Thirst" as an example, we can explore the beauty of this collection's title through three aspects: the cover, dedication, and ultimately, the examination of the title itself and its aesthetics.

The observer of the "Caravan of Thirst" collection finds within its cover five intricately intertwined elements, forming a precise depiction void of any discordance. The cover constitutes a complete artistic painting in its elements, expressing the essence of the events within the short story collection. It embodies dramatic elements that give the painting vitality and dynamism. Upon closer inspection, the emotional state of the creator is reflected in the painting, inducing a sense of interactive integration in the reader's mind, making the painting appear to move in sync with the events within the short story collection.

The five elements composing the cover's painting are as follows:

1. The right eye of the storyteller.
2. The title presented in two colors, yellow and white.
3. An image of two camels led by a single shepherd.
4. A drawing of a heart over the sands, with traces of two bare feet pointing towards it.

5. The background dominated by crimson red, with a hint of dusk-like color beneath the painting.

The first element, the storyteller's eye, reveals a longing gaze filled with ambition to quench the thirst for life's fountain. It symbolizes a struggle between the forbidden and the intense desire to surpass these restrictions. This blue-eyed gaze carries water-like qualities, quenching the thirsty, similar to water's ability to satisfy and alleviate thirst.

The second element, the title in two colors, yellow and white, signifies the desert's symbolism of aridity and harshness in the choice of the yellow color for "Caravan" while the white color in "Thirst" symbolizes quenching thirst in this desert landscape. The word "Thirst" is larger than "Caravan," symbolizing an enduring thirst, not merely for water but for emotional and sentimental fulfillment, hinting at the theme of love.

The third element in the cover image depicts two camels with a shepherd walking alongside them, holding the reins of the caravan. The fourth element, a heart drawn on the sand with two bare footprints nearby, suggests the longing and aspirations for satisfaction while the bare feet symbolize a genuine effort to break free from emotional constraints, aiming to alleviate the longing that corrodes the hearts.

The cover's symbolic elements vividly portray the quest to quench an eternal thirst, not just for water but for emotional satisfaction, symbolizing a heartfelt journey toward liberation from emotional barriers and the desire to extinguish the thirst that plagues the hearts.

The fifth element on the cover, the crimson red color dominating the background except for a small area tinged with a dusk-like shade, carries many implications pertinent to the text's context. In this collection, the red color signifies human thirst, manifested through love and physical satisfaction. The slightly smirking lip depicted on the cover is a subtle detail noticed only by those who carefully examine the painting. Lips are a symbol of kissing and are known as messengers of love, quenching thirst and yearning in the realm of affection. The unified and harmonious interplay of elements on the cover, with their vivid aesthetics, places the reader in front of the focal point around which the events in this short story collection revolve.

The Dedication:

The dedication represents a threshold encapsulating the writer's vision, revealing cognitive and emotional facets through concise, eloquent sentences. It frames the high rhetoric and succinctness prevalent in the narrative. The dedication in this collection is expressed in an intriguing manner through a declarative phrase that initiates the dedication, stating: "How thirsty are those who do not know they are thirsty." It uses linguistic paradox to express astonishment at the intensity of people's thirst, with the irony lying in their unawareness of their own thirst. This paradox serves to surprise the reader, prompting an exploration of the dedication's beauty and aligning with the writer's support of those innocents who don't recognize their thirst. The dedication, opening the author's collection, forms the core of this literary work, becoming the hub where fragmented narratives from the stories within the collection converge.

The Title Sentence "Caravan of Thirst":

The title forms the core of any literary work, serving as the key to access the structural elements constituting the aesthetic meaning in the literary text. The selection of a title is not arbitrary or random; it embodies the essence of the writer's work. The choice of the title is based on works closest to the writer's inner self, expressing the psychological, personal, and cultural facets comprehensively within the stories of the collection. In the collection by the storyteller (Sanaa Al-Shalhan) currently in discussion, "Caravan of Thirst" stands as the ideal choice for the collection's identity. It also represents the first story leading the collection, encapsulating the writer's vision that permeates all the collection's narratives. The writer reveals her perspective on the lives of the impoverished and unfortunate, who are enveloped in thirst, yet not for water but for love's emotions and sentiments. The beauty of the title resides in the word "Caravan." Traditionally, caravans traversing deserts primarily carry water. However, the writer, through the title, transforms this caravan into an encyclopedia of thirst, filling people with impassioned love but leaving them in perpetual thirst due to societal taboos. The "Caravan of Thirst" journeyed not for water but for love, inadvertently carrying the unquenched thirst for affection. This excerpt from the story titled "Caravan of Thirst" reveals the writer's vision, illustrating a thirst for love and passion, a void that every human strives to fulfill with the noble emotion of love.

The short story collection "Caravan of Thirst" consists of fifteen stories, starting with "Caravan of Thirst" and concluding with "The Body". The writer managed to create imaginative titles for the stories, forming a circular pattern where the first story's core aligns with the final one, interconnecting the stories in between with delicate threads that bind the elements of the collection.

"Caravan of Thirst" takes the reader on a journey, unveiling a society that deprives individuals of their basic rights, offering energy to femininity and a desire for waiting. This story serves as a starting point. "A Message to God" portrays desire and complaint while contemplating divine duty.

"The Rag" presents a tale brimming with intense emotions, showcasing how unfamiliar entities can harbor powerful feelings, while humans continue their existence without experiencing such sentiments.

"Heart for All Bodies" narrates the story of a woman in search of genuine love, yet her heart remains empty as she finds love in everyone, ultimately circling back to the starting point.

"The Envy" concludes the collection with a story depicting an eternal search, where the person remains in a perpetual state of waiting. The caravan retraces its journey in the pursuit of the ideal body, continuing in a cycle without reaching a haven of stability.

The writer's imagination blends with rich emotions to craft texts brimming with feelings and passion. The stories revisit the beginning and end in an endless loop, leaving the reader with a sense of continuous and eternal anticipation.

The collection "Caravan of Thirst" by the author Sanaa Al Shaalan is a captivating assemblage of fifteen stories, each intricately woven to create a tapestry of emotions, themes, and interconnected narratives. This collection delves deep into the complexities of human emotions, relationships, and the eternal pursuit of love.

At its outset, the story "Caravan of Thirst"

introduces readers to a society constrained by societal norms, highlighting the deprivation of fundamental human needs while embracing the energy of femininity and the art of waiting. This story serves as the nucleus, around which the other narratives orbit.

"A Message to God" poignantly portrays the desperation and yearning that is often met with rejection. This story reflects on the divine and the limitations of its response to human pleas, illustrating how such impassioned appeals often remain unheard.

"The Rag" introduces an intriguing notion wherein non-human entities possess emotions far more intense than many humans. It juxtaposes the existence of these powerful feelings with the apathy or lack of such sentiments in humans, creating a thought-provoking dichotomy.

"Heart for All Bodies" follows the journey of a woman seeking pure and authentic love, yet consistently finding it in everyone she encounters, leading to an inevitable return to the starting point of her quest.

Finally, "The Envy" concludes the collection, echoing the theme of eternal search and unfulfilled desires. This story poignantly reflects on the perpetual state of yearning and anticipation, symbolized by the caravan's ceaseless quest for the ideal body.

The writer's masterful storytelling intertwines rich emotions, passionate narratives, and thought-provoking themes throughout the collection. Each story in "Caravan of Thirst" contributes to a cyclical pattern, echoing the journey of longing and seeking fulfillment, only to return to the starting point, leaving the reader with a lingering sense of perpetual anticipation and unresolved desires.

Through these stories, Sanaa Al Shaalan offers readers a profound exploration of the human condition, relationships, and the enduring pursuit of love. The collection serves as a reflective mirror, inviting readers to contemplate the depths of their own emotions and the eternal quest for fulfillment in life.

.

Conclusion:

"Caravan of Thirst" transcends the ordinary boundaries of storytelling, immersing readers in a realm of emotional depth and contemplation. Sanaa Al Shaalan's collection resonates with the essence of human longing, portraying characters entangled in the intricate web of desires, love, and unfulfilled aspirations.

As the caravan of stories unfolds, each tale becomes a chapter in the grand narrative of human emotions. Through vivid prose and profound storytelling, Al Shaalan offers a poignant reflection on the human condition, inviting readers to traverse the realms of longing, love, and the relentless pursuit of contentment. This collection serves as a mirror, reflecting the intricacies of the human soul, leaving readers with a lingering contemplation of their own yearnings and the perennial quest for fulfillment in life.

Bibliography

Al-Attas, S. M. N. (1993). Islam and secularism. Kuala Lumpur: ISTAC.

Al-Dimasyqi, A.-I. A.-N. (2016). Syarh Shahih Muslim. Dar al-Kutub al-`Ilmiyah.

Allen, C. (2013). Islamophobia. In Islamophobia. https://doi.org/10.4324/9781315745077-41

al-Maraghi, M. (2002). Tafsir al-Maraghi. Beirut: Darul Fikir.

Al-Qaradawi, Y. (2010). Islam an introduction. Kuala Lumpur: Islamic Book Trust.

al-Qurtubi, A. A. M. ibn A. (2014). Tafsir al-Qurtubi (Vol. 20). Beirut: Dar al-Kutub al-'Ilmiyah.

Al-Qushayri, I. (2018). Tafsir al-Qushayri. Dar Ihya' al-Turath al-Arabi.

Al-Rāzī, F. (2000). Al-Tafsīr al-Kabīr aw Mafātih al-Gayb, Vol. VII. Dar Al-Hadith.

Al-Sya'rawi, A.-I. A.-M. (2007). Tafsir Al-Sya'rawi.

Qitha' al-Saqafah wa al-Kutub.

Al-Syawkani, M. bin A. (2014). Fath al-Qadir al-Jami' baina Fannai al-Riwayah wa al-Dirayah min 'Ilm al-Tafsir, Vol. 5. Dar Ibnu Hazim.

Al-Thabathaba'i. (1987). Tafsir Al-Mizan. Islamic Publications Office.

Al-Zuhaily, W. (2009). Al-Tafsir al-Munir fi al-Aqidah wa al-Syariah wa al-Manhaj. Dar al-Fikr.

APS (Applied Social Psychology). (2017). The Role of Religion in Prejudice Enablement and Reduction. Retrieved December 26, 2022, from https://sites.psu.edu/aspsy/2017/09/28/the-role-of-religion-in-prejudice-enablement-and-reduction/

Bakhshi Hazrat 'Alī Aḥmed and Rizwānur Raḥmān. (2012). Glimpses of the Holy Qur'ān. (New Delhi: Adam Publishers and Distributors).

Chelini-Pont, B. (2013). Relationship between Stereotyping and the Place of Religion in the Public Sphere. In J. Svartvik, Jesper & Wiren (Ed.), Religious Stereotyping and Interreligious Relations (pp. 75–84). Palgrave Macmillan.

Geertz, C. (1977). The Interpretation of Cultures. Basic Books.

Geertz, C. (2013). Religion as a cultural system. In Anthropological Approaches to the Study of Religion (pp. 1–46). https://doi.org/10.4324/9781315017570

Hanafi, H. (2000). Islam in the modern world: Religion, ideology and development vol. I. Cairo: Dar Kabaa.

Hanafi, H. (2006). Culture and civilizations, conflict or dialogue? Vol. I the meridian thought. Cairo: Book Center for Publishing.

Jafari, F. (2020). Theological knowledge in Islamic mysticism and gnosticism." Kanz Philosophia A Journal for Islamic Philosophy and Mysticism 6(2). DOI: https://doi.org/10.20871/kpjipm.v6i2.92.

Karama, M. J., & Khater, N. A. (2020). Educational peace theory in the holy qur'an. Al-Bayān – Journal of Qurʾān and Ḥadīth Studies, 18, 138–154.

http://scholar.ppu.edu/bitstream/handle/12345678
9/2214/1.pdf?sequence=1&isAllowed=y

Khairulnizam, M., & Saili, S. (2009). Inter-faith dialogue: The qur'anic and prophetic perspective. Journal of Usuluddin, 9(2), 65–94.

Khaldun, I. (2015). Muqaddimah. Cairo: Dar-Ibnu al-Aitam.

Kidwai, Salim. (1996). Hindustani Mufassirein Awr Unki' Arabi Tafsirein (in Urdu) .(New Delhi:Maktaba Jamiah).

Kokan, Moḥammad Yousuf. (1960). Arabic and Persian in Carnatic, (Madras: Hafiza House).

Ma'roof M M M. (1995). *Spoken Tamil dialect of the Muslims of Sri Lanka: Language as Identity classifier.* Islamic Studies 34 (4).

Nashir, H. (2015). Understanding the ideology of Muhammadiyah. Muhammadiyah University Press.

Nieuwkerk, K. van, LeVine, M., & Stokes, M. (2016). Islam and popular culture. University of Texas Press.

Patji, A. R. (1991). The Arabs of Surabaya: a study

of sociocultural integration. Canberra: Australian National University.

Putra, A. D., Purnomo, D., & Utomo, A. W. (2019). Sociological study of harmony in diversity: Lessons from Salatiga. Walisongo: Jurnal Penelitian Sosial Keagamaan, 27(1), 69–98. 10.21580/ws.27.1.3504

Ridwan, M., & Robikah, S. (2019). Ethical vision of the qur'an: Interpreting concept of the qur'anic sociology in developing religious harmony. Jurnal Ilmiah Islam Futura, 18(2), 308–326. http://dx.doi.org/10.22373/jiif.v19i2.5444

Sanaa Sha'lan, 'Adore Me'(A'shaquni), Daira al-Maktaba al- Wataniyya, Hashemite Kingdom of Jordan, Third Edition, 2016.
Shaalan, Sanaa, "Thirst Caravan Stories," Dar al-Waraq and Distribution/Jordan, 2006.

Saerozi, M. (2017). Dynamics of the development of istiqomah mosque in front of a church in Ungaran Central Java Indonesia. Journal of Indonesian Islam, 11(02), 423–458. 10.15642/JIIS.2017.11.2.423-458

Saged, A. A. (2021). Honoring the human self with a world peace study in the light of purposes the holy quran. Quranika: Journal of Libahuts Qur'an, 19(2), 223–234.

Shareef, Moḥammed Muṣṭafa and Bad'iuddin Ṣabri. (2008). Development of Tafseer Literature in India, (Hyderabad: Osmania University).

Shihab, M. Q. (2004). Tafsir al-mishbah. Jakarta: Lentera Hati.

Shu'aib, Tayka. (1993). Arabic, Arwi and Persian in Sarandib and Tamil Nadu, (Chennai: Imaamul Aroos Trust).
Thabari, I. J. (1999). Tafsir al Thabari. Kairo: Dar al Fikr.

Zamakhsyari, M. I. U. al. (2012). Al-kassyaf 'an haqaiq al-tanzil wa 'uyun al-ta'wil fi wujuh al-ta'wil. Cairo: Dar al-Hadis.

Zubair, K M A Aḥamed. (2010). *Tamil-Arabic Relationship*, ed. John Samuel G, (Chennai:The Institute of Asian Studies Press).

Zubair, K M A Ahamed. (2012). *Eminent Scholars of Sheik Sadaqathullah Appa's Family and their contribution to Arabic and Islamic Studies,* (in Arabic), Thaqafatul ḥind 54, (3&4).

Zubair, K M A Ahamed. (2013). *Qasaid al-Madaih al-Nabaviyya fi Tamil Nadu,* (in Arabic), Thaqafatul ḥind 64, (4).

Zubair, K M A Aḥamed. (2017). Prophet's Panegyrics in Arabic Literature, (Moldova: Lambert Academic Publishing).

Printed by Books on Demand GmbH, Norderstedt / Germany